Meet your emotions!

Fill in the missing words:

When my favourite toy breaks, I feel ....

When someone says something mean to me, I feel ....

When I see my friend that I haven't seen for ages, I feel ....

When I can't sleep in the dark room, I feel ....

When it's nearly my birthday, I feel ....

When I catch the smell of a bin, I feel ....

When someone gives me a hug, I feel ....

There are no right or wrong answers in this exercise! The things you might have written down - like sad, scared, happy - are called emotions.

God has given everybody emotions, and he has put them inside us to help us out in various ways.

In this book we will focus most on four core emotions:

JOY

SADNESS

ANGER

FEAR

Can you spot them in the picture?

I'm afraid you'll need to learn to handle us

I'm sad to say that sometimes we can behave in unhelpful ways

As emotions, we're not bad or good, we just are! We're here to help you work out what's going on in your life. Happy news, eh?

I need you to see us. And call us by our names. OK!?

EMOTIONS

You will also be able to spot some other emotions that might pop in from time to time in this book: **Excitement, Surprise, Shame, Curiosity and Disgust.**

Your emotions are a bit like a group of friends - sometimes one of them takes a lead and another follows; sometimes they get into conflicts and sometimes they play and have fun together!

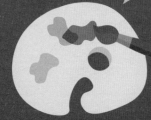

Your emotions are a bit like colours: just like mixing blue and red makes purple, the emotions can mix and be a little different at different times. There is no one palette of colour that is right for everybody all of the time.

3

The emotions on the previous page are shown as different colours. You may think of your emotions as other colours: that's fine!

Can you think about what emotions are swirling around inside you right now and try to draw them here or on a separate paper just using colours?

Don't feel the need to draw characters or write words, just use the colours to show how you feel.

Jesus and emotions

One thing we will discover in this book is that Jesus experienced the same emotions that we experience. In the Bible, it says that Jesus is able to feel sympathy for our weaknesses because he was tempted in every way like we are. That means he must have felt the temptation to do things like run away when he was scared, or hurt someone in anger, or gloat when he got something right, and so on. But even though he felt tempted to do those things, he resisted the temptation. He didn't let those feelings cause him to disobey God or hurt other people (Heb 4:15).

Jesus has told us many amazing things through the Bible, but he also *showed* us how to live. He showed us how to be fully human.

Praying your emotions

Like Anger said on the previous page, emotions can be a little attention-seeking at times: we need to notice them and call them by their names. It's helpful to notice our emotions together with our friends and families, perhaps around this book, or at bed- or meal-times. We can also talk to God about our emotions - he really wants us to chat to him about how we feel. Talking to him about these things is part of what we often call 'praying'.

The Psalms, the book of prayers and songs in the middle of the Bible, is stuffed full of emotions! We'll be using these to reflect and pray later on. Look at the colour drawing you did earlier on. Hold the picture in your hands and pray something like the prayer on the right.

"This is how I feel today, God. Thank you that you know what these emotions feel like, because Jesus felt them too. Amen."

JOY

Psalm 100 (a paraphrase)

Shout with joy to the Lord; everybody, everywhere!

Bring laughter as your worship to him,

Sing happy songs before him.

Get your head around that the Lord is God; he made us, we belong to him, he cares for us like farmers care for their flocks and herds.

Come before God with "Thank you!" on your lips; come close to him with celebration.

Yes! Sing thank-you songs and praise songs to God.

Because the Lord is all good, his love never fails, it goes on forever, he is faithful to you, and to your children, and to your children's children as well. Forever.

Over to you!

Use a coloured pen to circle any words in this psalm that make you think of Joy.

Use a different coloured pen to underline all the *reasons* listed for being happy.

The writer of this psalm says to shout, laugh and sing to express Joy. How do you show that you're happy?

I might make you feel all bubbly inside, give you a shot of energy and you might find that you can't help but smile.

I'm the feeling you get when you've reached a goal too, whether it's learning to write, cleaning the house or organising a meet-up with a friend – doesn't it feel good?

Over to you!

What does **Joy** usually feel like in *your* body?

I help you celebrate all the good things in life! My job is to help you relax and also bond with other people – I know you just love having a laugh with your friends, don't you?

When I'm too small in your life, you end up feeling stressed and tense and it's harder to be a good friend.

The Pursuit of Happiness

Everybody wants to be happy and many people state "happiness" as the goal of their lives. But we can't pursue happiness itself, we can only pursue what makes us happy. We all know people who pursue money or power, believing it will make them happy, only to end up with an empty life. There are some universal pursuits that are known to increase joy, like meaningful tasks, good relationships and creative expression. Ultimately, as Christians, we can see how these things fit in with following Jesus, and how pursuing God and his purposes for the world is the true source of joy (see Matt 6:28-34). How can you pursue God today?

Jesus is Happy (retelling of Luke 10:1-24)

There were crowds of happy people around Jesus wherever he went. Just imagine the joy of all those people being healed! Imagine not being able to walk (in a time before wheelchairs or cars), and then suddenly your legs being made well again. How would you react?

Another clue to Jesus being a smiley, happy person is how many times we read about him hanging out with children (for example, Matt 18:2, Mark 10:13 and Luke 9:47): Have you ever met a small child who likes being with someone grumpy or angry?

For a while Jesus had been teaching and training his friends in how to share the happy news he had come to bring. One day he decided that they knew enough. He rounded up seventy-two of them and told them to spread out to different villages to tell everybody about him.

How did Jesus spend his time waiting for them to come back? We don't know - perhaps he had a nap, because he was buzzing with energy when they eventually returned!

We are told that the seventy-two friends came back elated and happy.

"Lord," they exclaimed, *"When we used your name, even the evil spirits obeyed us and stopped hurting people!"* They were ecstatic, and Jesus looked at them proudly and lovingly.

"Evil doesn't stand a chance!" he replied, *"I've given you power, stronger than the enemy's. But that's nothing; the real joy is that God has signed you up for an eternity with him."*

Then Jesus laughed, filled up to the brim with happiness in the Holy Spirit, and he prayed a celebration prayer:

"I praise you, Father, ruler of heaven and earth, that you've hidden these things from those who think themselves so clever, but showed them to those who are childlike and innocent! Yes, that makes you happy, Father."

Later, when Jesus was alone with his friends he told them: *"You are such a fortunate bunch to see what you've seen. Many rulers and holy people could only dream of experiencing what you've just been through."*

Over to you!

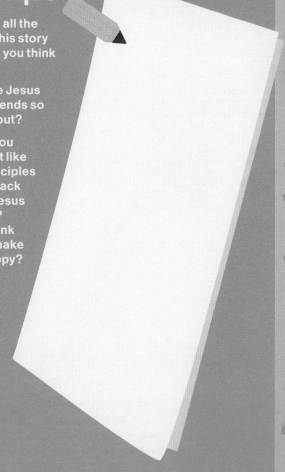

Underline all the words in this story that make you think of **Joy**.

What were Jesus and his friends so happy about?

What do you think it felt like for the disciples to come back and see Jesus so happy? Do you think that you make Jesus happy?

Simple Joy

Sometimes if we feel like we have too little Joy, we can help ourselves surprisingly easily. Our emotions don't just live in our minds - we feel our emotions with our whole bodies.

So sometimes we can help our emotions by caring for our bodies. Looking after yourself is not selfish, God made us to need these things.

HAPPY

What top 5 things make you feel happy?

1.

2.

3.

4.

5.

JOY & CURIOSITY

Joy and Curiosity are firm friends. Often, being curious about something will bring you Joy. For example, you might be curious about whether you could climb a big rock. If you manage to keep Fear at bay and have a go at the climb, the sense of achievement will make you feel Joy.

Jesus seemed to be one of the most curious people ever: he was constantly asking questions of the people around him! That might be one reason why he was so happy.

God's best for you

The following are some ideas for God's best for you, things that are less about fun moments, and more about things that make us feel good every day. They're so simple that they are worth trying, don't you think?

Draw a smiley face by things you already do and praying hands by the things you want to ask for God's help with:

 Get enough sleep and go to bed the same time every night.

 Get some exercise every day, even if it's just a short walk.

 Eat lots of fruit and vegetables that spread your energy out throughout the day.

 Cut down on screen-time, especially if you spend a lot of time with social media or news; much of what people put online is designed to make you outraged or upset.

 Human contact: ask someone for a hug or meet up with a friend. If you can't do that even a video chat will help!

 Do something creative! Try singing, dancing, knitting, building, drawing or whatever creative activity you enjoy.

Grown-up tips

Read the book *"Jesus Asked"* by Conrad Gempf to discover more about Jesus' curiosity.

Sometimes, if you are really happy and excited about something, someone might tell you to *"take it down a notch"*, or tell you to *"stop being so self-centred"*. Unfortunately, Shame may then swoop in and stop you from feeling Joy, because you think you did something wrong. This may feel like a sinking feeling in your stomach, or your face might feel warm.

If this is your experience, you may need to make friends again with Joy and Excitement. Like with all other emotions, this involves making time and space for them, and trying to sense in your body what they feel like.

When something happy happens, practise saying *"I'm feeling Joy right now!"* If someone in the family gets embarrassed by feeling happy or excited (perhaps they feel the urge to hide), help each other out by saying *"You're feeling excited, that's great!"* If the Excitement is hurting others by being very loud, perhaps suggest other ways of celebrating, like dancing, singing a song, developing your own goal-scoring celebration, or something else.

Celebration prayer

A lot of songs in church have very joyful words – which is your favourite praise song? God wants to hear about our happiness, just like he wants to hear about our other emotions. In the outline of the word HAPPY below, draw or doodle things about God that make you feel happy, but also all the little things of the life he has given you that bring you Joy too.

HAPPY

FEAR

Psalm 27 (a paraphrase)

The Lord is my torch in a dark room, and rescues me from danger – why should I be afraid? The Lord is an indestructible fortress – why should I tremble?

Those who run to attack me fall flat on their face. Even if a whole army surrounds me, my heart will not be scared.

The thing I long for most is to spend time in God's presence, to enjoy being near him. God's presence is my hiding place when trouble comes, he keeps me safe, out of reach from evil. Soon I will sing praise songs to God again!

Teach me how to live, O Lord, so that I don't go down a dangerous path. Danger lurks around the corner, but I know that you will keep me alive, God, and show your goodness to me while I live.

Stay with the Lord, in his presence. Be brave, and stay with the Lord.

Over to you!

How do you think the writer was feeling when this psalm was written?

Underline anything that would be comforting to you if you were scared.

What do you think the writer believes will help him / her be less fearful?

I make your body want to escape the danger, using the Fight, Flight or Freeze response. That's helpful when it comes to being attacked by a lion, but, I'm afraid, perhaps less helpful when it comes to sitting an exam, public speaking or telling someone how we feel – things that people are often scared of.

Over to you!

What does **Fear** usually feel like in *your* body?

You will feel me in your body in tense muscles, increased heart rate and either a sudden flow of energy or feeling faint. You might shake or get cold hands and feet and a dry mouth.

My job is to keep you out of danger. WATCH OUT!!

Jesus is Scared (retelling of Mark 14:32-42)

After Jesus had eaten the Last Supper with his friends, they went to a garden called Gethsemane, a favourite spot. They had just had a big meal and it was late, so Jesus' friends were yawning. But Jesus was not. He knew that danger was around the corner, so he wanted to pray. Jesus pointed his friends to a flat, comfy spot in the garden.

"Sit down here while I pray," he told them. Then he took his three closest friends, Peter, James and John, with him to a private spot. Jesus became very anxious and upset. *"I feel overwhelmed, it feels like death!"* he told them, *"Please stay and watch and pray!"*

Jesus went off a little further into the garden by himself, fell down on the ground and prayed for a way out: *"Dad, my Father, could you get me out of this?! But let your will be done, not mine!"*

When Jesus came back to his friends, they were not watching and praying, but had fallen asleep. Jesus had to wake them up, before going off and praying the same prayer over and over. Three times he prayed the same prayer, three times he had to wake his friends up.

But after the third time, they all had a rude awakening. Judas, one of their group of friends, showed himself a traitor, and had brought a violent crowd to come and arrest Jesus. The time for prayer was over, and Jesus willingly allowed them to take him away, while his friends ran away, afraid for their lives.

Over to you!

Circle or underline any words that make you think that Jesus felt scared.

Talk about why he was scared - was he right to feel scared?

Jesus shows us three ways to handle Fear:

1. Tell God
2. Tell our friends
3. Stay with the Fear until it calms down

Which of those could you do when you feel scared?

When to run away?

If we run away every time something scares us (for example, a spider) or avoid something that scares us (for example, going to sleep by ourselves) we teach our brains that this situation was in fact dangerous. It will make us more scared the next time we face the same thing. But when something is not dangerous, we can decide to not avoid it; to not run away immediately. If we stay with the scary thing a little bit longer each time, we will eventually learn that it's not dangerous. Distraction, like counting windows or listening to a song, is a good strategy if it helps us remain in the scary situation.

It's the grown-ups' job to teach children what is dangerous (like running out in front of a car) and what isn't (like making new friends), and model how to respond to such situations.

We saw in the story that Jesus didn't run away from the fear in Gethsemane, but stayed with it, together with friends, allowing his Father to calm him and strengthen him for the challenge ahead.

What is something that you're scared of that is not actually dangerous?

How can you stay with that Fear next time you feel it?

Strategies for staying with unnecessary Fear

Even if we know logically that something isn't dangerous, our bodies still feel scared. So, the first step is to use action to show our bodies that they're out of danger. Slow your breathing down, by breathing in on a count of three and out slowly on a count of four. Then get rid of the excess energy Fear put in your body (in case you needed to run away or fight!) by wiggling your body, doing some star jumps or having a dance!

For centuries, Christians have used breathing to pray. Have a go at a breathing prayer now! You could choose any words you want to pray, but for example, why not using the last line from Psalm 27? As you breath in, think the words *"Be brave"* and as you breathe out, say the rest of the words in your mind *"...and stay with the Lord."* Repeat this as many times as you like. This is less like a "please-God" prayer and more of a "being-with-God" prayer.

(See also 'Engage at Home', 30 March https://engageworship.org/EngageAtHome)

Introduce...

FEAR to CURIOSITY

Curiosity and Fear aren't really friends, because Fear keeps chasing Curiosity away! You might feel curious about what it's like to sing a solo at church, but Fear might stop you from ever having a go.

When we feel overwhelmed by Fear, it can be helpful to invite Curiosity in to ask some questions, like *"What are some tips and tricks for feeling confident when performing?"*, or - if you're scared of spiders - *"I wonder how spiders catch their food?"* or - if you're scared of injections - *"How does this vaccine work?"*

Unmasking Fear

Fear is scared of everything, especially being seen and noticed. It often dresses up as a different emotion, especially Anger, to avoid being seen. When someone expresses Anger, it can be helpful to keep in mind that they might really be feeling Fear.

Can you think of an example when someone in your family has expressed Anger, but really felt Fear?

At other times, Fear might hide behind Shame. Someone might have told you that only babies get scared, and instead of feeling the Fear you need in a scary situation, you feel Shame, because you don't want to be childish.

We need to unmask Fear, and use the strategies above to stay with it.

An example could be if a child gets momentarily lost. The grown-up might get really angry with the child, even though they were really afraid.

This may involve chatting and helping each other – that's OK! Praying doesn't have to be quiet or still.

A folding prayer around Fear

1. Find a piece of blank paper and fold it up twice.

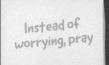

Instead of worrying, pray

2. Write Phil 4:6 (MSG) on the folded paper: *"Instead of worrying, pray."*

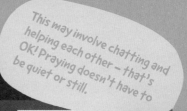

Favourite Psalm 27 line

3. Turn the folded paper over and write your favourite line from Psalm 27 (see page 9). Read these out as the beginning of your prayer.

Anger & Shame....

4. Unfold your paper and write Anger and Shame at the top. Is there anything you feel Anger or Shame about right now? Say, write or draw these to God.

Fear...

5. Lower down, write Fear. Are there things that you know that you are fearful of? Or can you look under the surface of the Anger and the Shame to see if it might be Fear lurking there? Say, write or draw these things to God.

Jesus

6. Finally open the paper up fully and write Jesus in the middle. You could either just take your time over writing the name "Jesus" and simply be in the moment; you could doodle and draw about Jesus around his name or you could write thank-you prayers to Jesus for helping us carry our Fear. Rest in God's presence.

SURPRISE

I'm a very short-lived emotion, I just pop in before you decide what to feel about something.

There's a story in the Bible of Jesus being surprised. A leader in the Roman army had a servant that was ill. Not all of the Romans posted in the area were very popular, but this man was. He seemed to be seeking God, and had even built a synagogue - a Jewish place for prayer - for the locals. He heard the stories about this teacher who could heal people, so he sent some of his Jewish friends to ask Jesus if he might heal the servant. Jesus agreed and began walking with the friends towards the Roman's house, but before he could get there, a messenger came to meet him. This was his message from the Roman army man:

"Don't come to my house, I don't deserve it! I don't even deserve to come and talk to you in person! But as a leader in an army, I know about orders; when I tell my soldiers to 'go' they go. You can just give that order for the illness to go away, and I know it will!"

Jesus was surprised when he heard this, he couldn't believe his ears. He turned to the crowd that was following him and exclaimed:

"Such amazing faith! And this from a Roman! I've not seen such a remarkable faith in anyone else!" When the messengers returned home, they found that the servant was well again. (Luke 7:1-10)

I appear briefly when something happens that you don't know immediately what to feel about – for example, if you unwrap a gift, or someone jumps out at you from behind a tree. I'll lead you to the right emotion, like Joy or Fear.

Over to you!

What does Surprise usually feel like in *your* body?

In this frame draw a picture of Jesus' surprised face:

Surprised by God's love

We can get surprised when something isn't as we expected it. Sometimes we don't expect God to be 100% kind and loving toward us, since that is so out of our experience as humans. None of us can show loving kindness to another all of the time. But God can. We can allow God to Surprise us with his love again and again. It's the kind of Surprise that brings us Joy. Draw and doodle around these Bible verses about God's surprising love for us. Perhaps circle words that are surprising or special to you. Take some time to let the Surprise change to Joy.

What marvellous love the Father has extended to us! Just look at it — we're called children of God! That's who we really are.
(1 John 3:1 MSG)

Jesus said: "I've loved you the way my Father has loved me. Make yourselves at home in my love."
(John 15:9 MSG)

SADNESS

Psalm 42
(from The Message version)

I want to drink deep draughts of God. I'm thirsty for God—alive... I'm on a diet of tears - tears for breakfast, tears for supper. All day long people knock at my door, pestering, "Where is this God of yours?"

These are the things I go over and over, emptying out the pockets of my life. I was always at the head of the worshipping crowd, right out in front, leading them all, eager to arrive and worship, shouting praises, singing thanksgiving - celebrating, all of us, God's feast!

Why are you down in the dumps, dear soul? Why are you crying the blues? Fix my eyes on God - soon I'll be praising again. He puts a smile on my face. He's my God.

When my soul is in the dumps, I rehearse everything I know of you ...

Sometimes I ask God, my rock-solid God, "Why did you let me down? Why am I walking around in tears, harassed by enemies?"...

Why are you down in the dumps, dear soul? Why are you crying the blues? Fix my eyes on God - soon I'll be praising again. He puts a smile on my face. He's my God.

Over to you!

What does **Sadness** usually feel like in *your* body?

Over to you!

Highlight any words that make you think the writer felt sad.

What was she / he sad about? Do you ever feel sad without really knowing why?

Do you think it's OK to suggest that God has let us down?

How is the writer trying to bring Joy back into her / his life?

My job is to help you deal with, and get your brain used to, loss. I will come and help if you lose something you love; a toy, a best friend or even a grandparent. Loss isn't always about things, we also sometimes lose hope or Joy.

I often make you feel tired and low in energy. Sometimes I will make you feel droopy – it's your body's way to stop you from distracting yourself with activity. Instead, it's time to reflect.

If you force yourself to cheer up when you're feeling sad, I will just pop up at another time. You need to spend some time with me before things will feel better.

Jesus is Sad (retelling of John 11:1-44)

Mary, Martha and their brother Lazarus were some of Jesus' very best friends. They had shared many meals, laughs and chats together. But one day Lazarus became seriously ill. The sisters knew that Jesus loved Lazarus and would want to know of his sickness. They also knew that Jesus had the power to heal him. So they sent a message to Jesus letting him know that his friend was ill. At the time, Jesus had left his friends' area, Judea, to escape people who wanted to harm him. Despite this, Jesus took a couple of days to think about it, and then told his disciples that they were all heading back to Judea. His disciples were not happy, it would be dangerous to go back!

Now, Lazarus died and had been dead for several days by the time Jesus got near to his home. Martha went out to meet Jesus in private.

"Jesus, if you had been here, my brother would not have died!" Martha exclaimed, *"But I believe that you are the King, sent from God."* Jesus spoke to her about life and death and that believing in him meant rising again, even if our bodies die. Then Martha went to fetch her sister.

Mary was very upset, she fell down in a heap by Jesus' feet and cried: *"Jesus, if you had been here, my brother wouldn't have died!"*

When Jesus saw Mary weeping, he felt so sad too, and he wept. Both of them crying, Mary showed Jesus where Lazarus' body had been buried in a cave.

"Open the grave," Jesus asked the people around him. *"But Jesus,"* Martha objected, *"Lazarus has been dead for several days!"*

"If you believe in me," Jesus replied, *"you'll see the amazing things God can do."*

Then Jesus prayed a prayer out loud, and shouted his friend's name: *"Lazarus! Lazarus, come out!"* Suddenly Lazarus, fully alive and well, came walking out of the grave, and all those who watched couldn't help but believe that Jesus was God's Son!

Over to you!

Underline or circle any words that show emotions.

How did Martha and Mary express their sadness differently?

Why do you think Jesus wept even though he knew Lazarus would come back to life?

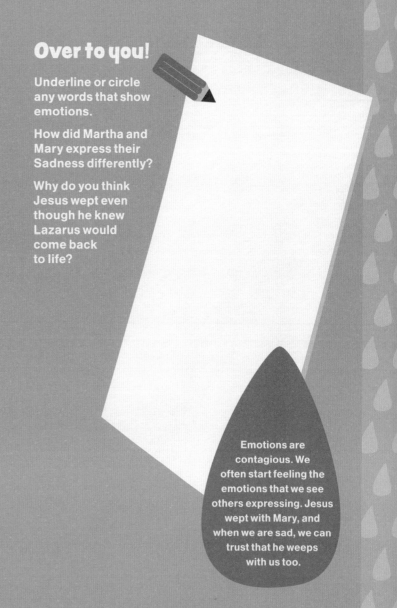

Emotions are contagious. We often start feeling the emotions that we see others expressing. Jesus wept with Mary, and when we are sad, we can trust that he weeps with us too.

How do you reflect?

Sadness tells us that it's time to think and reflect. How do you do that best when you feel sad? Different people in the family will have different ways to be sad and to reflect, for example crying, going for a walk, sitting outside alone, journalling, singing or listening to sad songs, having a cuddle, drawing and so on.

Talk about how each of you can express and reflect on Sadness best and write or draw it here:

The Bible verse below tells us that God is with us when we feel sad. Colour in and decorate the verse, and while you do that talk about what it might mean for God to be with us in our Sadness.

"The Lord is close to the brokenhearted; he rescues those whose spirits are crushed."

(Psalm 34:18 NLT)

Riding the waves of Sadness

When we feel sad, we often feel sad in waves. It starts with a really strong feeling, that comes back time and again, but after a while, the feeling becomes less strong and further apart. This is how our brain gets used to the thing that happened to make us sad.

It's important to remember that in between the waves, it's good to allow yourself to feel happy or excited. It's normal to then feel sad again later, but at least your body has had a little break from Sadness.

Thankfulness – an anchor in the waves

When we're bobbing on high waves of Sadness, we can throw down the anchor of thankfulness to stop us losing our way.

We are sad because we *don't* have something anymore, but we can be thankful for something we *do* have. For example, I'm sad that my holiday got cancelled, but I'm thankful for my lovely home. Psychologists tell us today how important thankfulness is for feeling well, but God, of course, already knew that! The Bible is full of encouragements to thank God for everything in our lives (look, for example, at Psalm 118, 1 Thess 5:18 and Phil 4:6).

Use these circles to help you pray "thank you" prayers:

God, I feel sad about:

...but I also feel thankful for:

150 words for emotions

Here are lots of words describing emotions. Some are big words: pick out a few and talk about - or look up - what they mean. Can you think of which of the core emotions they are most like? Circle the words with the colour of their emotion character. You may use this page at any time you feel something to help you work out exactly what you're feeling and to know which words to use to describe your emotion.

vengeful depressed resigned distressed discontent queasy homesick apprehension elated greedy exuberant satisfied panic bliss guilt earnest spellbound agitation exasperated hopeless open gloomy amazement generous agony alienation contempt awe cruel peaceful sorrow isolated adore envious subdued threatening gloating humiliated displeasure repentant grouchy afraid glad shock enraptured fondness bored pessimistic delighted eager cautious euphoria loathing frustrated weary optimistic enthusiasm enraged ferocious grim mad outrage alarmed defeated enthralled dismay dread timidity pensive spite tense amusement passive stressed thrilled interested lonely furious aggressive jealous jubilant insecure enjoying calm jolly enchanted annoyed anguished revulsion irritated compliant nervous scared raptured complacent disappointment proud disenchanted upset sympathetic triumphant pleased horror scorn merry disturbed bitter blue astonishment terror resentment fascinated content anxiety grief glum disillusioned serene remorse longing concerned misery relief embarrassed grumpy ecstatic wrath assertive stingy frightened mortified infatuated pity smug flustered keen tranquil happy cheerful composed sorry dissatisfied anticipation needy rage hostile wonder exhausted jaded unhappy

Emotion tracker

Day 4
Day 7
Day 3
Day 6
Day 1
Day 5
Day 2

Spend a week keeping track of what emotions you are feeling. Use some of the words from above if you like, or colour each day in the emotion characters' colours. Perhaps make trackers on a separate piece of paper for everyone in the family?

ANGER

Psalm 12 (a paraphrase)

Quick, God, I need your help! There seem to be no good people around anymore. Everyone is just lying all the time, planning mean tricks in their hearts.

Make them quiet, God! Zip their mean lips shut, stop their lying tongues from moving! They think they rule the world with their false words.

The poor and needy groan in prayer, and God responds: "Enough is enough! I will protect!"

There's nothing false in God's words: they are pure and true like silver and gold.

You, God, will keep the needy safe and will protect us forever from evil; those who are strutting about, getting away with lying and cheating.

Over to you!

Underline anything that shows the writer of this psalm being angry.

What was she / he angry about?

What do you think God feels about this prayer?

Would you ever pray anything like this?

Over to you!

What does **Anger** usually feel like in *your* body?

My job is to protect you and your boundaries. For example, if someone takes something that is yours, I'll remind you to say "No!" or if someone says something mean to you, I'll remind you to say "Stop!"

I will not go away until you notice me! It even helps to just say: "This makes me feel really angry!" Saying that you're angry is not bad. If you don't notice me, I might try even harder to get your attention, and people or things might get hurt...

You will notice me in your body in tense muscles, clenched jaw, your heart beating faster and your breathing speeding up.

Jesus is Angry (retelling of Mark 10:13-16)

One day, Jesus was sitting down, teaching his followers. As always there were crowds milling around; curious people, people who needed help, people who wanted to catch Jesus out. Lots of families were there too, with kids running around, playing hide-and-seek behind their parents tunics and shawls. The parents wanted the best for their kids, so decided to bring them up to Jesus.

"Please, Jesus, place your hands on my children and bless them!" they asked. They had seen Jesus bring healing and life to those he had touched, and who wouldn't want that for their kids? But Jesus' closest friends told them off!

"Do you think Jesus has time for your kids?" sneered Peter.

"He has much more important things to do!" exclaimed John.

"Don't interrupt the teacher!" said James, and told them to go to the back of the crowd.

But Jesus saw what was happening, and he got angry! *"What are you doing stopping the kids from coming to me?"* Jesus asked his friends indignantly, *"Don't stop them! It's for people like them that I've come!"* He gave his friends a final frustrated look, *"In fact, and this is the truth, if you don't come to me like a child, you won't be able to come at all!"*

While his friends scratched their beards, and felt a bit bad for being told off and wondered what he meant, Jesus gathered up the kids in his arms. He blessed them, spoke joy into their lives, and perhaps joined in with a game of peak-a-boo too.

Over to you!

Highlight the words that show how Jesus felt.

Why was Jesus angry?

Was there anything bad about his Anger?

Jesus' Anger is never selfish. His Anger is an expression of his love.

Love expression

Sometimes our Anger is an expression of our love, just like Jesus' Anger is. For example, if you love a friend, you get angry when someone is mean to them. Or if you love the earth God made, you get angry when people pollute or litter. The more we love what God loves, the more our Anger will be like Jesus' Anger.

> Think of one thing where your love might cause you to feel Anger, and draw that in the heart.

ANGER & CURIOSITY

When Anger and Curiosity decide to teamwork, we can change the world for the better.

> I'm angry that some people in our town don't have homes. I will work with Curiosity to work out what we can do about it!

> **Chatting to God** is a good time to express your Anger. Anger gets seen and God can handle it!

Taking care of Anger

Since Anger always wants your full attention, we need to practise saying

"Hi!"

and perhaps also

"Goodbye!"

to Anger.

Do a role-playing exercise together:

★ Take turns to remember something that makes you angry; for example, someone using your toy without asking first, or someone making a mess where you've just tidied up.

★ Practice using words to say what made you angry, for example *"I feel angry when you take my toys without asking"* or *"I feel angry about the chocolate stains in the sofa."*

★ Everyone in the conversation should now give Anger the attention it wants. Say something like *"I can see that this makes you angry"* or *"I notice the Anger"*. Don't ever laugh at Anger, it will make it bigger: just notice it.

★ It might be that once everyone has said *"Hi!"* to Anger, you start feeling less angry. This is an invitation to talk about boundaries: do we have the same boundaries as a family? Examples of boundaries might be: *"these are the toys I don't want other people to touch without asking"* or *"the living room is out of bounds for eating, food has to stay on the dining table"* or *"knock before entering someone's bedroom"* or whatever else causes conflict and Anger in your family. Can we agree where the boundaries go?

★ It might be that someone needs to ask for forgiveness for overstepping someone else's boundaries.

★ After that, Anger probably has had all the attention it needed, and you can say *"Goodbye!"* together.

Grown-up tips

Remember that other emotions like fear and sadness might hide behind anger! Ask each other questions to find out which emotion is at the root of the display of anger, and make sure to notice whatever is hiding underneath.

Fighting back!

If we feel angry because a lion is invading our village it might be helpful to feel a rush of adrenaline and a need to fight back. This response is less helpful if you feel Anger about, for example, someone calling you names at school.

Fighting back hurts people, but it's good to find ways to get rid of all the energy in your body when you feel Anger. Sports and exercise are particularly helpful for this.

Circle what you think might be your best way to move your body when you feel angry.

Anger in others

If someone is angry with you, how do you feel?
Circle your experience:

I feel Shame and apologise even if I haven't done anything wrong

I feel Sad and start to cry

I feel Anger and want to fight back

I feel Fear and run away

I feel ....
(fill in your own words)

Talk in your family about how you each experience other people's Anger. Talk about which responses feel OK, and how each of you ideally would like an angry situation to play out. How can we avoid hurting each other or damaging property? What are words that help us become friends again? Draw or doodle the thoughts about your chat here:

Praying with Anger

1 God, I feel angry about…

2 God, this is what I want you to do about it…

3 God, is there anything you want me to do about this?
(be curious about the Anger)

EXCITEMENT

In your body, I can feel like your heart beating faster and your breathing getting quicker, and I might give you butterflies in your stomach.

I like mingling with other emotions, and when I visit I don't stay for very long (if I did, you'd get really stressed!)

I work a lot with Curiosity to get you asking questions and to get your creative juices flowing.

I work a lot with Joy as I give you the potential to reach a goal.

Over to you!

What does Excitement usually feel like in *your* body?

I'm not the best emotion to have around when you need to make good decisions...

Sometimes I work with Fear, like in the Excitement of going on a scary ride in a theme park, and sometimes I hang out with Anger, like when you get all energised about getting back at your sibling for something they did. I'm not always helpful then...

Excited in worship

God is definitely worth getting excited about, but when we worship him in church, it's sometimes not so exciting. When we do get excited, we get lots of extra energy in our body, and it feels good to use that energy by moving. These are verses from Psalms about different ways to worship God. Could you make up actions or dance moves to these verses and worship God excitedly?

"Clap your hands, everyone, everywhere: shout to God with happy shouts, because God is awesome, ruler over all the earth!"

(Psalm 47:1)

"Let's bow down low in worship, let's fall on our knees before God the Creator, because he looks after us."

(Psalm 95:6–7)

"Make the noise of the sea, of the whole earth, clap your hands with the rivers, sing together with the mountains, let the whole earth sing to our true and just God."

(Psalm 98:7–9)

"Sing a new song to God – praise him! Praise him with dancing, with the jangle of the tambourine and the strumming of the strings."

(Psalm 149:1, 3)

23

DISGUST

My job is to protect you from things that will harm you; like food that has gone bad or things that are toxic, whether it's something germy or someone who wants to harm you.

In your body, I can feel like sickness in your stomach, and you might automatically pull a grimace, scrunching up your face.

I make you reject things that repulse you, by making you say 'no' or – if it's really serious – throwing up.

I might work with Anger, for example if someone brings you something that makes you feel Disgust.

Over to you!

What does **Disgust** usually feel like in *your* body?

Disgusting injustice

We can feel moral Disgust, for example when we learn about the conditions of workers involved in modern-day slavery or another injustice. We should listen to Disgust and let it call us to pray and act on behalf of those who are oppressed. This is what God said to the people of Israel, through the prophet Amos (5:21-24), when they were oppressing the weak and the poor:

"I'm disgusted by your celebrations, I can't stand your meetings. Get the sound of your singing away from me! But let justice roll on like a river, truth and right-living like an endless stream!"

Use this space to pray for things that are not just or right. Allow yourself to feel disgusted about the injustice, and ask God to change the situation:

Grown-up tips

We need to be careful about making children over-ride their feelings of disgust. Even though it matters little in the case of, for example, broccoli - they will need disgust to keep them safe throughout their lives.

SHAME

Psalm 51 (Paraphrase)

Quick, God, I need your help!
Have mercy on me, God,
because your love never fails.
Because you are so compassionate,
clean away the stain of my sin.
Wash me clean from my guilt,
scrub my sin away.

I know I have done wrong,
I can't stop thinking about it!
It's against you I have done wrong,
that's what really matters.
You know what's right and what's wrong,
you are right to point out the wrong I did.
I've done wrong for a long time.

But I know you want honesty from me.
Only you can clean away my sin,
you are better than any soap.
Oh, give me back my joy again!
Give me a new, baby-pure heart,
help me be faithful to you;
don't push me away!

Help me follow your right way,
then I can lead others along.
Forgive me that I might sing again,
unseal my lips to praise you.
You're not looking for a life that
looks good on the outside;
the perfect words or songs in church.
What you want is an honest, sorry and
broken heart.
You will not turn away a sorry heart.

Over to you!

What is the writer
asking God for?

Underline anything
that shows that the
writer is lacking Joy.

David wrote this
psalm after he had
snatched another
man's wife and then
arranged for the
man to be killed in
battle. How is David
feeling about what
he has done? Do
you think God can
forgive something
like that?

Sometimes I'm good and healthy,
but that's only when there is guilt
involved – when you've actually
done something wrong. My task
then is to get you to try to undo
your wrong by apologising and
fixing anything that can be fixed.
That's how to get Joy back, there
are no shortcuts.

Sometimes I'm toxic
and unhealthy – you
really should not
listen to me then!
Toxic Shame tells you
that your whole
being is wrong, and it
doesn't involve any
actual guilt. Some
people struggle with
Toxic Shame their
whole lives, but Jesus
does not want that
for us.*

Over to you!

What does **Shame**
usually feel like
in *your* body?

You might feel me
in your body as an
urge to hide or you
might feel your
face go hot.

My job is to let you
know if you've done
something that
hurts others.

 **Grown-up tips**

*Some disagree that there is such a thing as "healthy shame", and would rather call the productive version "guilt" and
the toxic version "shame". Brené Brown has done lots of good work on shame which you might find helpful. Our description
here is a simple representation of a complex emotion. Toxic shame is the root of many psychological problems we may
suffer, and it's one of those things that is easily passed on between generations. You may want to research this for yourself
and don't be afraid to ask for help. A life lived without toxic shame is light and free!

KYLA'S SHAME

To help us understand what the Bible says about Shame, let's begin with a story of a little girl and her Mum:

Kyla was allowed to play with anything in the living room, except the vase. Her Mum had been really clear: *"That vase is very delicate and old, you mustn't touch it."* But Kyla found it so pretty, so unusual, and she knew that if she just picked it up one time there wouldn't be a problem...

"CRASH!" Oh no, what could Kyla do? The vase was in three pieces, so she ran to get some sticky tape. After a little repair work, with the broken part facing the wall, she thought Mum probably wouldn't notice...

Mum immediately noticed. Her face went very still as she turned to Kyla and said sharply: *"What happened with my vase?!"* Before Mum could say anything else, Kyla bolted up the stairs, slammed her bedroom door and hid under the covers. Her face felt all hot and her heart was beating really fast - she just wanted to disappear, but there was nowhere to go and so she burst into big sobs.

After what seemed like an eternity, the door opened gently. Mum sat down on the bed and slowly pulled back the covers to reveal Kyla's red, tear-stained face. *"Kyla honey, you knew that vase meant a lot to me. You disobeyed me. That makes me feel sad. But the truth is, you are more important to me than a vase. There are some things in life we can't fix with sticky tape. There are things we can't fix by running and hiding. The important thing here is that you and I fix our relationship. How do you think we can do that?"*

"I don't know Mum. I really am so sorry, but I just feel awful for breaking your vase, and I know that even if I spent all my pocket money I couldn't buy another one just like it. And... I'm scared you will always be angry and never forgive me."

Mum looked at her with concern and love. *"What you're feeling, Kyla, is called Shame. But relationships aren't like vases. They can be mended, when one person says they are sorry and the other person chooses to forgive them. Both of those things are hard to do, they are costly. But you've said you're sorry, and I've chosen to forgive you."* Both Mum and Kyla were smiling now. *"I love you Kyla, and I would pay any price to forgive you."*

Over to you!

What does it feel like to be **forgiven**?

Jesus and our Shame

The Bible says that the first humans started out feeling no Shame (Gen 2:25). When they disobeyed God, they felt Shame, and tried to fix it by covering themselves with fig leaves. Then they tried to hide from God (Gen 3:7-8). It was a lot like Kyla, trying to fix the vase and then hide from her Mum.

Jesus is the only person who never needed to feel Shame, because he always obeyed God and lived out God's best for him. But the amazing thing is that Jesus did choose to feel your Shame - yours, mine, the whole world's Shame. He embraced the shameful death of hanging on a cross, the most humiliating and disgracing experience you could imagine. He took on his shoulders the Shame of the whole world.

And because of this, he also experienced our broken relationship with Father God. He was cut off from the one he'd known and loved for eternity. On the cross he cried out *"My God, why have you left me alone?"* (Matt 27:46) He paid the cost of saying *"I'm sorry"* and the cost of saying *"You are forgiven"*.

Because of this, we do not need to be ashamed. Jesus has been raised from death and we can share in his Shame-free life. We don't need to try and fix our Shame, or hide from God or other people. More than Kyla's Mum or our earthly parents could ever do, God went to the greatest lengths to wipe away our Shame and restore our relationship with him.

"God didn't go to all the trouble of sending his Son merely to point an accusing finger, telling the world how bad it was. He came to help, to put the world right again."
John 3:17 | MSG

"Keep your eyes on Jesus, our leader and instructor. He was willing to die a shameful death on the cross because of the joy he knew would be his afterwards; and now he sits in the place of honour by the throne of God."
Heb 12:2 | TLB

Over to you!

Talk about ways you can help each other remember to turn to Jesus when you feel Shame.

How to apologise

We can pray and ask God to forgive us when we disobey him, and he will. But when we have done something that hurts other people, it's really important that we try to mend any resulting broken relationships. We need to apologise to people we hurt, even though it feels uncomfortable. Here are some useful tips on how to apologise (these are from Dr Harriet Lerner's book "*Why Won't You Apologize*"):

- ★ Never use the word 'but' in your apology
- ★ Talk about what you have done, not the other person
- ★ Offer to replace or repay anything lost, if that's possible
- ★ One sincere apology is enough

- ★ Don't talk about who started it
- ★ An apology is only worth something if you try your hardest not to offend again
- ★ Don't demand that the other person does anything, not even forgive
- ★ A sincere apology should never make the other person feel worse

> Remember, even if you sometimes do things that are wrong, **you yourself are not wrong.** God loves you so very much, and you are fearfully and wonderfully made! (Ps 139:14). He wants to be really close to you and take care of you.

Dealing with Shame in prayer

Follow this flow chart:

Are you feeling Shame? → **Yes** → **Have you done something wrong?** → **Yes** → **Did you hurt someone else?**

Are you feeling Shame? → **No**

Have you done something wrong? → **No** → You don't need to feel Shame if you have not done anything wrong.

Did you hurt someone else? → **No** → Tell God what you did and ask for forgiveness.

Did you hurt someone else? → **Yes** → Go and apologise (even if it's in a letter) and make amends if possible, and then come back.

You don't need to feel Shame if you have not done anything wrong. → Shake off the feelings of Shame, perhaps wriggling your arms and legs a bit.

Go and apologise... → Tell God what you did and ask for forgiveness.

Shake off the feelings of Shame... → Know that God accepts you! The Bible says that "*...now, those who are in Christ Jesus are not judged guilty.*" (Rom 8:1)

No (from Are you feeling Shame?) → Know that God accepts you! The Bible says that "*...now, those who are in Christ Jesus are not judged guilty.*" (Rom 8:1)

Tell God what you did and ask for forgiveness. → Pray a prayer of thanks!

A life of healthy emotions

Psalm 16 (a paraphrase)

Protect me God, I want to hide in you. You are better than every other good thing in my life. You have given me what I need, no more, no less, my life is good and pleasant, I delight in all you've given to me.

I praise the Lord, who advises me always, even into the night you guide my heart. I fix my eyes on the Lord, with you by my side I won't be shaken.

And so; I'm happy in my heart, I sing cheerful songs, and my body feels secure and at rest. Because I know you will never leave me, I will always have your life within me.

You show me the way I should go, and I'm content when I'm near you, for eternity I'll be happy in your presence.

Over to you!

Underline any words that show how the writer feels.

Circle any words or phrases that show *why* they feel like they do.

Pick one phrase you'd like to be able to say in a prayer, and write it here:

As followers of Jesus, we want to become more like him. We can learn from Jesus' life how to have a healthy relationship with our emotions. We've explored in this book how emotions are good gifts from God, given to help guide and protect us. Can you draw lines to match the emotion with its function?

SADNESS   JOY   FEAR   ANGER   SHAME   DISGUST   EXCITEMENT

| Stops us engaging with things that will be bad for us | Protects us from danger | Helps us know when we've hurt someone | Helps us let go of things we lose | Makes us curious to learn new things | Helps us know when things are right and connects us with others | Helps us protect our boundaries |

Sometimes, one or two of our emotions can become too big or too small, and we end up hurting others or feeling bad about ourselves. Can you think of ways your emotions might have got involved in unhelpful behaviour in the past?

Experiencing the fullness of God

It's important that we come to God with whatever emotions we are feeling. We often come to him with Joy, and we experience our wonderful, loving, generous God. But if we only ever come to him when we are happy, we will never get to know the God of comfort meeting us in our Sadness, the God of forgiveness and healing meeting us in our Shame, the God of justice meeting us in our Anger and the God of protection meeting us in our Fear.

Using the colours of our emotion characters, colour in this shape of a person (if you want to do more than one drawing, create your own outlines on plain paper). Think about what emotions you have and where you might feel these in your body. What would be a healthy amount of each different emotion? Colour in this outline to think about what emotional health might look like for you.